PLAYS

by

Norman Giddan

and

Jane Giddan

Cult Classics Publisher

Dallas, Texas

USA

PLAYS

by

Norman Giddan

and

Jane Giddan

Cult Classics Publisher

Dallas Texas

USA

Copyright 2018 by Norman Giddan

All Rights Reserved

Cult Classics Publisher

1613 A Black Duck Terrace

Carrollton, TX 75010

www.culclassicspublisher.com

ISBN-13: 978-0-9981068-4-7

ISBN-10: 0998106844

Library of Congress Catalog Number: 2018944533

Printed in the USA

CONTENTS

INTRODUCTION

These plays contain a mixture of humans and birds – mostly grackles.

While there are some magnificent species in the world of birds, grackles are more-or-less ordinary, though fortunately capable of heroism when their dreams lead them to reach for the sky. They love human beings, but also have suffered because of them. They eat waste grain after a harvest and grow fat. Dire consequences follow the urbanization of their natural habitat. So, civilization has been a mixed bag for grackles as they struggle to survive and multiply.

Grackles are blackbirds, yet distinctively iridescent black; some with a purplish head and bronze body. All peer at the world through striking yellow eyes. They forage for seeds or grain, prefer small fish or mice, and many types of invertebrates.

Their songs and calls are harsh and sharp; they nest in small trees with a clutch of one to seven eggs. Long, keel-shaped tails immediately signal their presence. Bird-watchers usually ignore grackles.

Survival

A Play for Elementary School

by

Norman and Jane Giddan

CAST

Ma Grackle

Pa Grackle

Wise Elder #1

Wise Elder #2

Buzzy Buzzard

Bertie Buzzard

Freddie Flax – boy – age 9

Eddie Eagle

Pilot Pigeon

SETTINGS

Scene 1

Farm

Freddie Flax: Safe flight, Pilot Pigeon. You carry an important message…inviting grackles to tonight's harvest *(claps his hands)*.

Pilot Pigeon: No worry, Freddie. Never had a problem on this route.

Freddie Flax: Grackles are starving…love seeing you fly in.

Pilot Pigeon: I'll fly fast. Got to help them survive *(tests his wings)*.

(Pigeon dead in farm's field)

Bertie Buzzard: Some dumb duck hunter shot it by mistake. Didn't know his birds.

Buzzy Buzzard: Pigeon is delicious. So tender and juicy.

Bertie Buzzard: Must have been a carrier pigeon. What does it say?

Buzzy Buzzard: "Hello, Grackles. Harvest is tonight. Come and feast. Your friend, Freddie Flax."

Bertie Buzzard: Let's not tell the grackles. We'll tell the sparrows. They could use a big meal, too.

Buzzy Buzzard: Grackles may not make it. They're starving to death.

Bertie Buzzard: I love grackle flesh…after it rots *(stands erect with head up)*.

Scene 2

Grackle habitat

Ma Grackle: Pa, I hope we can hold out *(walks very slowly)*.

Pa Grackle: Yep. Weak from hunger. Some older birds are...nearly dead.

Ma Grackle: There's no sign of Pilot Pigeon. Must be on his way. I hope he's okay. Freddie Flax always comes through for us. Such a good kid. And he's only nine years old.

Pa Grackle: It's so hard not to get frustrated. I'm to the point where I'd steal food, to help our flock *(sighs heavily)*. Can't wait much longer. Pilot Pigeon's not coming. We need food badly *(struts slowly, with tail dragging)*.

Ma Grackle: Our group that flew to Farmer Flax's field has returned—empty handed. Our grain and seeds have been eaten...field is picked clean.

Pa Grackle: Why didn't Freddie Flax tell us about the harvest? Can't he be trusted? I'm so disappointed and angry at him.

Ma Grackle: Maybe Pilot Pigeon had an accident or got sick *(puts wing around Pa, to console him)*.

Scene 3

Search party

Pa Grackle: Half a dozen of us birds are strong enough to fly. We'll go search for Pilot Pigeon *(they fly away)*.

Ma Grackle: Look over there, Pa *(points her beak)*. Those are pigeon bones.

Pa Grackle: *(lands near bones)* There's a note. Must have been in the leg-band. Buzzards ate everything.

Ma Grackle: Buzzards didn't tell us about the harvest. They knew from this note. I'll bet they told the sparrows. I hate them *(pecks at ground)*.

Pa Grackle: They want us. They know we're weak and starving…make a tasty meal for them. Now we know that Freddie is on our side. He wouldn't betray us *(smiles with satisfaction)*.

Buzzy Buzzard: Come on, Bertie, let's swoop low and scare them *(flies fast at grackles)*.

Bertie Buzzard: You little black birds can't even get off the ground. You're pitiful *(feigns chewing on flesh)*.

Pa Grackle: Two awful buzzards. Get out of here.

Bertie Buzzard: Still hungry? Sparrows had a wonderful feast.

Ma Grackle: Leave us alone. You took our food. You're so selfish. It was ours. Freddie always leaves it for us.

Buzzy Buzzard: We'll be back. You can count on it *(flies off into dark clouds, thunder and lightning)*.

Scene 4

Elder Council

Pa Grackle: We're the elder council. Supposed to be wise. We need a miracle.

Freddie: I'm little but I know survival is your goal. Don't strike back against the buzzards. I hate them too. They ate Pilot Pigeon. The sparrows took your food. You usually get to my family's field first.

Pa Grackle: We could steal the sacks of grain from the sparrows. It's ours.

Ma Grackle: Forget it, guys, at least for now. We need better communication than a single carrier pigeon. Right now we need to eat!

Freddie: Maybe bugs and worms could get you through this tough time.

(Search party for food)

Pa Grackle: Freddie had a good idea. We flew here. I'm exhausted.

Ma Grackle: Me, too. I've had two small worms to eat. Now I need to rest *(leans against the tree trunk).*

Pa Grackle: Look at our flock…so tired and weak. Can't even dig very well.

Ma Grackle: There is an Old West saying: "If your stomach is empty, it feeds on sorrow." That's me, Pa. I'm just plain sad. *(Pa wraps his wings around her).*

Scene 5

Elder Council

Wise Elder #1: A guy rode shotgun to protect the stagecoach in the Old West.

Wise Elder #2: Early trains had armed soldiers to protect the gold and other valuables.

Pa Grackle: Okay. Okay. We need to protect the pigeons. We all agree *(nods head impatiently)*.

Freddie: Don't laugh at me. How about an eagle to bring messages? A big, beautiful eagle. I could help train one.

(Several hours later)

Ma Grackle: Very nice of you to fly here, Eddie, especially on such short notice *(smiles, weakly)*.

Eddie Eagle: Always been fond of you little black birds. How can I help?

Pa Grackle: We're starving. We need food. Our supply didn't work out—our carrier pigeon was killed. Could eagles become our couriers? No one would bother them.

Eddie Eagle: *(preens his huge body)* We might help with your enemies. Eagles aren't meant to be couriers—we don't do that. Sorry *(flies off with loud flapping of wings)*.

Ma Grackle: We tried. Freddie might have another idea up his sleeve. He's our only hope, young but very smart.

Scene 6

Grackle habitat

Ma Grackle: I hear a tractor coming, Pa.

Pa Grackle: I knew Freddie would come through. I never really lost faith in him *(both fly to him).*

Ma Grackle: *(takes the note from Freddie Flax)* Here's his note. "Tonight. Our other field." And on the flip side, "We'll bring bags of grain and seed."

Pa Grackle: Hooray! Another chance. We will survive! Thank you. We're so grateful, Freddie Flax…to you and your family.

Ma Grackle: Yes, we are so very thankful for your help. You've rescued us.

Pa Grackle: Let us know if you ever need us to clear pests out of your fields. We owe you *(both Ma and Pa flap wings in appreciation).*

Freddie Flax: May not be fair to others…grackles are my favorites *(pats heads of grackles, who perch on door of tractor).*

Scene 7

Pilot Pigeon memorial service

Ma Grackle: We've lost a real friend. A great helper for our flock *(head down)*.

Pa Grackle: Yes, goodbye Pilot Pigeon. Sleep well and rest easy. The duck hunter shot you by mistake. Your son, Pilot Pigeon, Jr. can replace you—with protection.

Wise Elder #1: We'll never let a pigeon fly alone with harvest information. Never again.

Wise Elder #2: Sooner or later, Buzzy and Bertie Buzzard will pay for their crime. They withheld information. It could have saved us. Those little sparrows were just lucky—in the right place, at the right time *(preens gray feathers on chest)*.

Scene 8

Farm

Pa Grackle: It's a pleasure to see the flock eating again *(smiles)*.

Ma Grackle: Yes. The field has lots of seed and grain—leftover from second harvest.

Pa Grackle: Freddie's family have been very kind and generous to us. Prepared sacks of grain for our weeks ahead *(sighs with relief)*.

Ma Grackle: We've learned some important lessons from all this:

-Never let carrier pigeon travel alone.

-Provide them with strong escorts.

-Have them stay in touch, throughout their journey.

-We can outsmart those buzzards without a war.

Pa Grackle: Oh yes. The sparrows are not to blame. It wasn't their idea to steal our food, though of course, they did well in this harvest.

Ma Grackle: Later on, let's talk to Freddie and our flock about some kind of sharing agreement with the sparrows. After all, they're birds, too! *(walks wing-in-wing with Pa)*.

Pa Grackle: Now, for our final goodbye to those buzzards, Buzzy and Bertie *(squats)*.

Ma Grackle: If we pretend to look weak and sick—here on the ground—they'll hover over us. Imagining a tasty meal.

Pa Grackle: On my signal. Everyone fly up together. NOW!

        (All grackles rise in unison and scare off the buzzards).

All: Yeah! Hooray! Hip! Hip! Hooray for Freddie Flax!

(Freddie Flax sits in the tractor and observes the grackles scaring off the buzzards).

Freddie: I love those grackles. Such tough little guys. Hope I grow up to be like them.

Kidnapped

A Play for Elementary School

by

Norman and Jane Giddan

CAST

Pa Grackle

Ma Grackle

Gregory Grackle – 10 years old

Greta Grackle – 8 years old

Victor Vulture

Vivian Vulture

Members of the flock

SETTINGS

Scene 1	Roof of hotel
Scene 2	Hotel lobby
Scene 3	Posse searches
Scene 4	Trap set
Scene 5	Vultures refuse reward
Scene 6	Vultures apologize

Roof of hotel

Ma: It's very slippery on this wet roof. No time to call for help. The ceiling of our hotel lobby is leaking. Got to fix this hole, quickly, before the next storm.

Pa: Hand me that stone, Greta. I'll add a wooden support beam to hold together the leavers and feathers…cover the opening.

Ma: *(holds umbrella over Pa)* Be careful you don't slide off. You know how the children worry.

Pa: If we had big, sharp claws like the vultures, we wouldn't have to worry about sliding off. We could dig into the straw with a tight grip. Hold our ground.

Greta: We're nearly finished, Pa. Another big storm. Hear the thunder? Dark clouds fill the sky.

(Argue with vultures who fly over the hotel)

Ma: Maybe we should go inside. Rain is so heavy. And the thunder.

Pa: Yes, let's go. We'll come up here later when the weather is better.

Ma: *(lightning)* Pa, I've been hit. It feels like I'm on fire. Help! Someone help us. Please help us!

Greta: I'll fly up there. I can help. Stay calm.

Victor: *(swoops to roof, quickly)* We've got you, little ones. We've got you. We got here first.

Vivian: I'll take Ma. You take Pa *(fly off, holding grackles)*.

Pa Grackle: We have as much right as you vultures to eat in the wetlands. Why force us to leave? You scare us.

Victor Vulture: Too bad, little ones. We're big. We need more to eat. You don't eat the same things we eat.

Ma Grackle: You vultures think because you're so strong, you can do whatever you want. Underneath the dead flesh you eat…the bugs and tiny fish and grain we like.

Vivian Vulture: Boo hoo. Boo hoo. Victor and I fly where we want. Eat what we want. Don't have to arrange meals for little black birds like your flock *(vultures fly away as rain starts)*.

Scene 2

Hotel lobby

Gregory: It's wet in here. The lobby holds many of us. Thank you for coming.

Greta: Don't be so polite. Our parents have been kidnapped…by two huge vultures. Lightning nearly killed them. I went for help. I'm so worried about them.

Gregory: They were working on the roof. Storm hit. They're too old. They wouldn't listen *(shakes head)*.

Greta: Are they still alive or not? Maybe horrible Victor and Vivian have already…We've got to make a plan. We've got to find them, soon.

Gregory: Where are they? Force might do it. A reward might be better. They'd release Ma and Pa. Who will volunteer to be in a posse—to find them? *(many wings flutter)*.

Gregory: Good. That's great. Let's go with the youngest. Strongest volunteers.

Greta: Good idea.

Scene 3

Posse searches

Greta: We've searched everywhere. Inside caves. The bottom of ponds.

Gregory: We can't give up.

Greta: Are those bones on the hillside *(gasps, as she lands near them)*.

Gregory: They're not bird bones. Please. Please. Please. Not bird bones.

Greta: No. They're from squirrels or field mice. Picked over by the vultures. Still plenty of hope. I love them so much *(sighs)*.

Scene 4

Trap set

Greta: Talked to the head of the bird area…at the zoo. We'll set a trap.

Gregory: Yes. What about bait?

Greta: Good question. We'll set a yummy trap for Victor and Vivian. They love to eat.

Gregory: But what?

Greta: The zoo guy said old flesh. Smells and looks like it's spoiled. Perfect for vultures. They deserve it.

Gregory: They also love it *(hops up and down gleefully)*.

(Bait trap)

Greta: Spoiled and stinks. Who would eat it? Only vultures *(closes mouth and holds her breath)*.

Gregory: This desert is a perfect place for this trap. We can see and hear them. They can't see or hear us.

Greta: Right. We'll hide in the hills and caves. We'll get those vultures. They'll have to return Ma and Pa. Those bullies. I hate them *(pecks at the desert sand)*. I hate them.

Scene 5

Vultures refuse reward

Vivian: Here's a note with this delicious meal. There's a big reward. All the flesh we want to eat, for six months…we give Ma and Pa back. It's not enough. Those grackles are cheap.

Victor: Ma and Pa might taste good, later, *(laughter)* after they age a bit.

Vivian: I wish they were bigger, with more meat—and not quite so fresh.

Victor: Right. Now, this is a wonderful meal, here. Plenty of meat, very old and spoiled. I feel like a true vulture.

(Ma and Pa are alive, blindfolded and shackled to some trees, close by, with beaks wired shut, so they can't make sounds or talk).

Vivian: Better check on Ma and Pa.

Victor: *(struts to trees)* How are you, little guys? So quiet. Hungry? Thirsty? *(shouts to Vivian).* They're fine. Burned here and there, but quite alive.

(Net covers vultures)

Gregory: *(net thrown around vultures)* This net should hold you two. You'll never kidnap grackles again. We hate you.

Victor: Let us go. We're innocent. We didn't hurt anyone. They're alive, over by the trees.

Greta: You're criminals. Back to face justice *(walks quickly to trees and releases Ma and Pa. They hug and wrap wings around each other with strong emotion).*

Vivian: Please let us be free. The net hurts. We can't fly. Our wings are trapped. We'll be your friends. We'll help you. Please. Please.

Gregory: Sorry, vultures. Back to a cage. That's where you belong. You'll get a fair trial.

Greta: *(to parents as she unties beaks)* Thank goodness you're alive. We'll get you help.

Pa: *(tests his wings)* I'm so glad you found us. We'll fly to the hospital. Get these scoundrels behind bars. To think our young daughter led the posse.

Ma: *(crying)* One more hug, Greta, and Gregory. One more before we leave.

Greta: Life imprisonment in a cage. That's their punishment. Guilty as charged.

Scene 6

Vultures apologize

At an appreciation service for Ma and Pa's recovery from their burns and injuries, Greta and Gregory reminisce lovingly about their parents. A recording is played of Victor and Vivian apologizing, stating that they thought Ma and Pa were alive and well. Flock weeps, unsure whether the apology is true or genuine.

Greta: Ma and Pa are everything to us. Fed us. Educated us. Helped us *(crying)*.

Gregory: We love them. I hope they know that. If they were gone…we'd feel so alone and sad.

Recording of Victor and Vivian speaking: "We are so sorry and apologize to the entire grackle flock. We thought Ma and Pa were safe. We should have been more careful. We are very, very sorry this happened."

Greta: I don't believe it.

Gregory: It's very convenient. Leave their cage. Be free. Never.

Pa: Thank you all, for your kind words *(wing wrapped around Ma)*. We love you all. We'll be around for a long time. Even if the vultures thought we were fine, what were they going to do with us? *(rubs tummy with foot)*.

Against the background of all the birds in the story, a small committee of wise vultures and wise grackles, which reports to Greta, establishes the Grackle Birdstop Educational Center to honor Ma and Pa. Purpose is to increase the understanding, appreciation, and living standards of all manner of birds, and to promote peace and justice among all of the species.

Greta: Thank you for establishing this Center. In the name of Ma and Pa. Wise birds have done this. We are very grateful

Gregory: Yes, we are. The Grackle Birdstop Educational Center is very important. We need peace and good will…among all types of birds. We need to help each other. Not fight.

Greta: We need to promote understanding. Improve the lives of all birds. No matter what species. Or where they live in the world.

ALL: *(in unison, with wings raised)* Gleeful bird noises.

Greta: *(to Ma and Pa)* It is my pleasure to give you, this bowl of leaves and grass. First material to be used in the Birdstop Center *(Ma and Pa wrap wings around each other, soundlessly).*

Bullying and Talking

A Play for Middle School

by

Norman and Jane Giddan

CAST

Pa Grayson: Middle School Teacher

Ma Grayson: Middle School Teacher

Greta Grayson: 6th grade

Gregory Grayson: 8th grade

Eddie Archer: 8th grade

Sally Silver: 8th grade

SETTINGS

Scene 1	Classroom
Scene 2	Classroom – essay
Scene 3	Soccer field
Scene 4	Grayson home
Scene 5	Soccer field
Scene 6	Grayson home

Scene 1

Classroom

Mr. and Mrs. Grayson, fortyish, co-teach fifteen children in a middle school classroom, in a small migrant community. Mixed age class, with children from various backgrounds. Science class is nearly over.

Mr. Grayson: This science class is so lively. Everybody's talking today *(walks around and smiles)*.

Mrs. Grayson: It's about the environment. That's important to all of us.

Mr. Grayson: It's fascinating to study ecology in our terrarium. Different species interact…the survival of all.

Greta: Fun to share our ideas.

Mrs. Grayson: So many different points of view. Each student has something unique to contribute.

Mr. Grayson: Like life in our terrarium. Their interactions keep our classroom so alive *(leans against large desk)*.

Mrs. Grayson: What do you think, Gregory?

Gregory: *(drums his fingers on desk)*.

Mr. Grayson: *(whispers to Mrs. Grayson)*. I'm so glad…left the big city to move here. Teaching is much more rewarding than running the hotel. Class dismissed.

(Students exit)

Mr. Grayson: What's up with Gregory? He hasn't been talking *(puts down pen)*.

Mrs. Grayson: We need to finish these lesson plans for tomorrow.

Mr. Grayson: I'm worried about him. Something's wrong *(rubs hand over bald head)*.

Mrs. Grayson: Let's see if we can figure out what's going on. It's not like Gregory to be so quiet.

Scene 2

Next science class

Mr. Grayson: Okay, class. Stop whispering, people. Listen up. We've got a great assignment for you *(puffs out chest)*.

Chorus: Oh, no!

Mrs. Grayson: You're to write a short essay on this topic: "Speak Up To Others."

Mr. Grayson: "What You've Always Wanted To Say To People." Stuff you've thought or felt. Haven't been able, or willing, to say.

Eddie: *(whines)* Oh, no. I hate to write.

Sally: Suffer, Eddie. Suffer *(sarcastic smile)*.

(Students write essays)

Mrs. Grayson: *(gasps)* Look at this, Pa. Gregory's telling us a lot in his assignment *(reading):*

"I'm good at the silent treatment, but it hasn't really helped very much. I get sick of being small, pushed around by the bigger guys."

"There are so many handsome boys that I don't have a chance with the girls, so I don't feel very good. I get scared a lot, and then I get very, very, very angry, but I know I shouldn't scream or hurt anybody. So I just clam up and don't say anything, especially to people like Eddie or Sally."

Mr. Grayson: What about his archrival, Eddie? *(stomps his foot)*.

Mrs. Grayson: Here's what Eddie writes:

"Even though I like to push the little guys around, I like some of them. Gregory's not a bad guy."

"I don't like being in class with all these babies. I need a little excitement to keep me interested. It's fun to scare the others and show them I'm the toughest. But, I don't mean to hurt anybody."

Mr. Grayson: There's some hope here *(hands together in mock prayer)*.

25

Mr. Grayson: *(walks up and down the aisle).* I am sick of the bullying. Several essays mentioned it.

Mrs. Grayson: We must treat each other with more respect.

Mr. Grayson: Bullying hurts everyone. The person who's targeted. The bully. Those of us who just stand by and watch *(punches the air).*

Mrs. Grayson: We want you to support each other. Gather around those who are bullied. Then just walk away, together. Come to us as a group. Let us know if mean things are going on. We will listen.

Mr. Grayson: *(loud)* Bullies need to know that they can change (lower voice after pause). They don't have to play that role. We'll help them find better ways to act.

Mrs. Grayson: We need a meeting with all of the parents, all of you students. Develop a program of action to stop and prevent all bullying.

Scene 3

Soccer field

Eddie: I just tripped you, little guy…Like that? *(sarcastic smile)*.

Mrs. Grayson: No more of that, Eddie.

Greta: We can still win, Gregory. Don't give up.

Eddie: Nobody can beat my team. We're the biggest and the best. Here's a little kick while I steal the soccer ball *(kicks Gregory)*. How do you feel about that? Ha ha.

Gregory: *(Ties his shoe)*.

Greta: I hate you Eddie Archer. I hate what you do to people.

Mr. Grayson: Game over. Eddie 12, Gregory 1. See you all tomorrow morning.

Eddie: Watch your step, Gregory. You're an endangered species.

Gregory: *(Runs across the field)*.

(Greta and friend Sally talk on sidelines).

Sally: Greta, I have such a crush on your brother. He's so cute *(sighs)*. What's going on…He's stopped talking to me.

Greta: He's changed, Sally. I love him dearly, but something's really wrong. It made me mad to see Eddie run right over him in the soccer match yesterday.

Sally: Eddie's a terrible bully, Greta. He loves to torment people.

Greta: Gregory should yell and scream at him—get really mad—or something. Not just take it. Not talk at all *(punches at air with free hand)*.

Scene 4

Grayson home living room

Mr. Grayson: *(pleads)* Gregory, we're all worried about you. What's wrong?

Gregory: *(looks down at the floor).*

Greta: I hate to see Eddie bullying you, Gregory. Tell him to stop *(cries).*

Mrs. Grayson: Gregory's not ready to talk about anything yet.

Mr. Grayson: We love you, Gregory. What can we do to help? Will you see a counselor? Or should I grab a wet noodle and beat some sense into you?

Gregory: *(silent).*

Mrs. Grayson: What about a psychiatrist?

Gregory: *(silent).*

Greta: Please, Gregory. Please do something. You can't go on like this *(cries with both hands on face).*

Gregory: *(leaves the room).*

(Grayson's alone)

Mrs. Grayson: I can't get things out of my mind. Gregory wasn't talking at school. Now he's stopped speaking when he's away from school.

Mr. Grayson: It's so strange that he participates in games, and does all his chores. Says nothing.

Mrs. Grayson: His silence makes him even more of a target of the bullies here. Won't defend himself.

Mr. Grayson: Maybe we shouldn't wait any longer to call in professional help.

Mrs. Grayson: Not before we try one more thing. I've got an idea that could work.

Scene 5

Soccer field

Mrs. Grayson: Gregory, we read your essay. Thank you for your honesty. I'm sorry you're so unhappy. I won't push you to talk right now. Here's a surprise…want you to know that Eddie says he likes you. Even wants to be your friend.

Mr. Grayson: Maybe if you meet him halfway, you two can find a way to be friends.

Gregory: Well, okay, Pa *(impulsively).* I'll give it a try. I thought he hated me.

Gregory: *(quietly walks away from Pa, and approaches Eddie).* Eddie, *(long pause, Gregory looks away)* can you help me learn how to be goalie?

Eddie: Sure, Gregory. Just because you're little, doesn't mean you can't be tough *(slaps Gregory on the back).*

(Eddie and Gregory work out with weights at soccer practice)

Eddie: *(stands behind Gregory).* Come on, little guy. You can do it. Lift those straight up twenty times.

Gregory: These weights are so heavy, Eddie. I don't know…

Eddie: Sure you can. Believe in yourself. Breathe each time *(demonstrates technique).*

Gregory: But I'll never be as strong as you are. You're so big.

Eddie: I'll kick your butt if you give up. Be as strong as you can be for your size. These workouts will strengthen your mind and your body. I'm still going to pick on you.

Gregory: *(poses in a boxer's stance).* I know you will. I'll figure out some clever way to fight back. I'm not going to let you bully me anymore.

Eddie: Well, we'll see about that, little guy. You're talking pretty tough. We'll see.

Scene 6

Grayson's home

Mrs. Grayson: How did it go with you and Eddie?

Gregory: We worked out together. When I'm afraid…I'm going to fight back.

Mrs. Grayson: You won't hurt him, will you? *(laughs).*

Gregory: No, but I'm going to do everything I can to stand up to him. He respects that. He hopes I'll stop letting people push me around *(broad smile).*

Mr. Grayson: So you won't be scared anymore?

Gregory: I won't always be nice to people. Sometimes I'll be scared. Sometimes mean and angry. I'll let them know how I feel *(raises voice).* I'll speak up.

Mrs. Grayson: Most of the time, you'll be nice *(puts arm around his shoulder).*

Gregory: Yeah, Ma. Don't worry. Most of the time I'll be nice.

Greta: Oh, it's so great to have you talking to us again. We all love you, big brother *(kisses his cheek).*

Mrs. Grayson: We sure do. More than you know.
Gregory: Me, too.

(Graysons' home)

Mrs. Grayson: Look how much fun the kids are having, Pa (waves arms as she dances).

Mr. Grayson: Yes, Ma. Eddie has sort of a date with Greta, and Gregory is dancing with Sally. What did you learn out of all of this?

Mrs. Grayson: Well, kids have to express what they feel. It's not always going to be nice. They'll learn to respect each other and themselves. Occasionally…they'll have disputes…all kinds of other feelings.

Mr. Grayson: It's a lot like our terrarium. Each person's behavior matters to the others. In turn, the whole community is affected (imitates hip-hop moves).

Mrs. Grayson: You are a fine teacher, my husband. Let's hope our class ecology stays healthy, and our students continue to bloom and blossom.

Secret

A Play for Middle School

by

Norman and Jane Giddan

CAST

Pa Grayson: Manager of hotel

Ma Grayson: Business Manager

Ginny Grayson: 6th grader

Gabe Grayson: 8th grader

Ms. Collins: 6th grade teacher

Mrs. Harmony: School counselor

Mr. Howard: Substitute teacher

SETTINGS

Scene 1	Hotel apartment
Scene 2	Hotel swimming pool
Scene 3	Computer email
Scene 4	Counselor
Scene 5	Medication
Scene 6	Diary
Scene 7	Graduation

Scene 1

Hotel apartment

Ginny: I won't go back there. Ever! *(pounds table)*.

Pa: Ginny, what is the matter? School is a good place. We all go to school. There's so much to learn.

Ginny: I hate it *(leaves the table)*.

Ma: Stay calm, sweetie, we'll work this out.

Gabe: I couldn't have gotten to eighth grade if I hadn't passed sixth. So there. You've got the same teacher, Ms. Collins. She's great, and pretty too.

(Later)

Ma: We talked to Ms. Collins. We're not going to force you to go, dear. We're here to help you.

Pa: Can you tell us why you won't go, Ginny?

Ginny: No, I can't *(serious and grim-faced)*.

Ma: It's okay. We'll home school you for a while. Ms. Collins will loan us books and assignments *(sips chili)*.

Ginny: Okay, I'll do that. Yes, that will be better *(takes big bite of salad)*.

Ma: Perhaps some counseling, too.

Ginny: Whatever.

Scene 2

Hotel swimming pool

Pa: Ginny, we know you like to go shopping or to the park. Why not school? Can you help us understand?

Ginny: I get teased at school for being little or dumb. It's embarrassing.

Ma: Okay, my, my *(rubs her back)*.

Ginny: I'm not as pretty or smart as the other girls. Beautiful girls—some from other countries. Ms. Collins is such a pretty lady, too. *(pulls herself over the side of the pool and stands on the patio)*.

Gabe: I get teased but then I fight them. *(flexes biceps)*.

Pa: You're beautiful, Ginny. I couldn't ask for a better or nicer daughter. Many girls have the same feelings you have. It's much more than the teasing. Isn't it?

Ginny: *(walks across patio, and dives into the swimming pool)*.

Scene 3

Computer email

Mrs. Harmony: Don't worry too much. I'll try to gradually reduce her fear. Let's help Ginny take "baby steps" back to school.

Ma: That sounds reassuring. I'm glad this is not permanent. I'd hate to think she won't go to college *(sighs heavily)*.

Pa: Now Ma, remember, she actually wants to be a teacher.

Mrs. Harmony: Why don't I visit with Ginny at your hotel? It might be easier for everyone.

Ma: That would be wonderful. Thank you so much, Mrs. Harmony. *(Ma and Pa hug, awkwardly, while still seated)*.

(Parents prepare)

Pa: This stuff isn't so easy, Ma. It's been going on a long time. *(walks around room, restlessly)*.

Ma: I know, dear, but home schooling is a step in the right direction. We can follow the assignments from Ms. Collins. Vocabulary words and definitions. Reading paragraphs and comprehension questions.

Pa: But the arithmetic and some of that spatial stuff. I can hardly do my checkbook *(shakes head in disgust)*.

Ma: Don't worry. I'll do the math. Remember my degree was in finance. I think this is pre-pre-algebra—just small equations *(thumbs through the book)*.

Pa: Good. I'll handle the assignment on space explorations. I'll have Ginny make a poster demonstrating what she understands about space and the astronauts. There must be something about that available on the Internet *(sits down at the computer)*.

(Parents teach)

Ginny: I don't want to do this. You're just like the teachers now.

Pa: Well, we have to be teachers if we home school.

Ginny: Whatever.

Ma: You need better topic sentences in your paragraphs. Come on strong and clear with them *(hands theme to Ginny, but she refuses)*.

Ginny: *(walks away)* I hate it. I don't like to write papers for school. It makes me too nervous.

Pa: Why are you so scared? It's just us. You, Ma, and me, helping you learn this stuff *(pleading tone)*.

Ginny: I don't want to study *(turns on TV)*.

Scene 4

Counselor

Ginny: I'm not crazy. I just do not…I just will not got back to school *(stomps feet)*.

Mrs. Harmony: I hear you loud and clear. School is a horrible place for you.

Ginny: Yes, it is. More than you could… *(eyes red and teary)*.

Mrs. Harmony: A lot of students think they'll fail. Or be criticized by the teacher. Not be able to compete. Do you?

Ginny: No.

Mrs. Harmony: So, it's something more specific. Perhaps a psychiatrist could help.

Ginny: Yes *(she runs along the path)*.

Scene 5

Medication

Ginny: Time for my happy pills, isn't it?

Ma: They'll help you relax, like the doctor said they would *(cuts lettuce)*.

Ginny: I'm not nuts. I don't need pills *(pretends to swallow several)*.

Ma: They'll help you decide to go back to school. Here, I'll make the salad dressing.

Ginny: They may hurt me. These pills could do bad things.

Ma: Dear, the doctor wouldn't have given them to you if they weren't safe.

Ginny: Pills are only for druggies or crazy people, not sixth graders like me *(pouts)*.

Ma: We'll read one of your favorite stories tonight. Wouldn't that be nice? *(tosses the salad)*.

Ginny: Whatever. Whatever.

Scene 6

Diary

Ma: *(read from diary, while emailing counselor)*. "Dear Diary—they'll never guess what happened to me. Everyone thinks I'm teased horribly or get bad grades on my schoolwork."

Pa: Yes, she's right.

Ma: "What if they knew about that teacher, Mr. Howard, who lives at our hotel part of the year—he's big and gruff."

Pa: I remember him. He's a substitute teacher.

Ma: "He did some awful things. He touched me in my private parts. I made him stop. I ran away." *(gasps)*.

Pa: Oh my God. I'll wring his neck *(face red)*. There are too many crazy people in this city. Horrible people.

Ma: "I hate teachers when they do that. He made me promise not to tell anyone." *(sobs and cries)*.

Mrs. Harmony: *(email)* You've done the right thing to send it to me. I'll be over to see Ginny tomorrow.

(Next day)

Ginny: I'm glad you know. Hard to keep such a big secret. I hate him.

Mrs. Harmony: He made you fear all teachers, maybe most of us adults, as well? *(puts arm around Ginny's shoulders)*.

Ginny: I've been so afraid. My stomach churns and I sweat. Sometimes I shake, too *(hands shake)*.

Mrs. Harmony: Your parents will report him to the school system and to the police. He'll be arrested.

Ginny: Yes. Yes. I want that, too. He's a bad man...to do what he did to a kid like me.

Mrs. Harmony: Yes.

Ginny: I'll probably always be a little scared.

Mrs. Harmony: That's perfectly normal. Maybe it'll make you more careful of who you're with and what you do.

(Next day)

Ginny: I feel much better about visiting school today. You've helped me a lot, Mrs. Harmony.

Mrs. Harmony: Thank you, Ginny. I'm glad you're feeling more comfortable. You're a good student. The other children like you.

Ginny: Mr. Howard called me to apologize *(angry tone)*. I hung up. I'll never ever talk to him.

Mrs. Harmony: His lawyer said he was guilty and the judge put him in prison for a long time. He needs help.

Ginny: He'll be punished. He deserves it. He can't hurt any more little kids like me.

Mrs. Harmony: You've been very courageous. All teachers aren't monsters, are they? *(opens arms to Ginny)*.

Ginny: No, most are just nice people. I feel so much safer now *(hugs Mrs. Harmony, and kisses her cheek)*.

Scene 7

Graduation

Ma: She looks so beautiful in that white dress *(tears run down face)*.

Pa: She's a real fighter. She overcame a big problem. Her honesty and ability to change are amazing.

Ma: I'm sorry it all happened, but she'll be stronger and smarter now.

Gabe: We all will. Things can happen to boys, too.

Pa: Friendships are such a big part of life, but we all have to be careful about who we choose to be with. Even nice neighbors or teachers can be a problem.

Ma: Ginny's getting her award. I'm so proud of our daughter. Here she comes.

Pa: She wants a fancy new cell phone *(stands up)*.

Ma: Maybe next year. Her old one still works. By the way, did Mr. Howard remember to pay his bill at the hotel, before he became a jailbird? *(stands up)*.

Ginny: *(runs down the aisle to her family and hugs and kissed each of them)*. I did it! I did it! Thank you. I love you.

Pa: Maybe we should move to a small town…safer for children.

Gangs Can Change

A Play for Young Teens

by

Norman and Jane Giddan

CAST

Pa Grayson

Ma Grayson

Gregory Grayson – 16

Greta Grayson – 14

Devils Gang Leader

Brady Birch – 16

Babs Birch – 14

Reds Gang Leader

Pa Birch

Ma Birch

Oliver Towles – Chief of Police

SETTINGS

Scene 1	Grayson home
Scene 2	Devils ceremony
Scene 3	Reds ceremony
Scene 4	Youth center
Scene 5	Birch home
Scene 6	Conference room
Scene 7	Conference room

Scene 1

Grayson home: Ma and Pa Grayson disturbed by two teenagers.

Ma Grayson: Where have we gone wrong, dear? Our two kids aren't...the same.

Pa Grayson: You're right. So rude. Won't follow our rules anymore.

Ma Grayson: I feel like kicking them out of the house...finish school somewhere else. Even our daughter, Greta...(*gasps*).

Pa Grayson: Neither one will listen to me, now. Not just becoming independent. Outright rebellion against everything we've taught them. I hate gangs.

Ma Grayson: It's like they have a new family. Different values and beliefs. We've been thrown away. College and good jobs are goals of the past. They don't need that horrible gang (*pounds hard on table in frustration*).

Scene 2

Greta and Gregory initiation ceremony into the Devils.

Devils Leader: Do you pledge complete loyalty to the death to the Devils?

Greta: Yes, I've got a tattoo on my lower back. A devil's head smiling (*nods head several times*).

Gregory: Yes, I pledge complete loyalty. I have shaved my head and had a ring set in my nose. (*points to it*) The word "devil" is embossed in the ring. Doesn't hurt anymore.

Devils Leader: We do things that your parents won't like.

Gregory: Yes, yes we know that. We'll follow orders. We'll be good gang members...no matter what.

Gang Members: (*chanting in unison*) New Devils! New Devils! Bad Devils! Bad Devils!

Devils Leader: Good. Let's have some fun tonight. Open up the keg of beer. We'll get drunk before we go out gang-banging. Let's review our plans for later.

(The Plan)

Greta: We'll do a drive-by, while the Reds are hiding or sleeping.

Gregory: I'll steal a car. Maybe some TV's or computers. Scare them.

Devils Leader: Imagine that I've grabbed a car door. No one's in it. Oops, a bunch of boxes fell out. I'm taking them.

Greta: Oh, Gregory, you probably can't start a car.

Devils Leader: Drive-bys can be dangerous to everyone. Part of gang life. You're both Devils now.

Scene 3

Brady and Babs Birch initiation into Reds

Babs Birch: I feel dizzy. I must be drunk…red berry wine we had to swallow (*sits down awkwardly*).

Brady Birch: Me, too. We're becoming Reds—a real gang. Like we'll have all these brothers and sisters.

Reds Leader: Enough, you two. Promise never to reveal any of our secrets or what we do. Tell no one.

Babs Birch: I promise. Stop that. (*touches head*) What are you doing to my hair?

Reds Leader: We're painting your hair with red dye. You'll look like red wine (*gang laughs*). Maybe taste like it, too.

Brady Birch: You're making me look like a druggie…all that red dye. I promise I'll never tell anyone.

Reds Leader: You're both accepted. Now, we'll finish this part of the initiation (*Gang members pour bottles of red wine over Babs and Brady*). Then we'll rehearse our next step.

Babs Birch: It's raining wine. Hurrah! We're in, Brady. (*smug tone*) We're in a gang.

Reds Leader: Here's our scenario. Memorize it.

(The Scenario)

Brady Birch: Devils deserve to be fought to the death.

Babs Birch: Do a drive-by and burn out front yards. That'll hurt the Devils.

Reds Leader: Use small torches. Drive in quickly. Light as much grass and bushes as you can.

Brady Birch: Good, Babs. You're really going to light the place up.

Babs Birch: I love planning the excitement of a drive-by like this. We can really scare old people to death if we cause enough trouble.

Reds Leader: Looks like you have. (*snickers*) Look at those two old folk over there.

46

Scene 4

Youth Center

Gregory: Stop it. Didn't you see what happens to gang members? They end up in prison.

Brady Birch: Who cares? Watch this, Babs *(throws gas canister)*. I'm angry at those dumb Devils. That'll hurt them, plenty.

Babs Birch: Right on, big brother. We're plenty tough. We're Reds...we're Reds...not the weak Devils.

Greta: *(runs straight at Babs)* Stop it, you dumb Reds.

Devils Leader: Attack, Devils, attack *(gang throws unlit Molotov cocktails at Reds)*.

Gregory: Oh, my leg has been hurt. I'm in pain, and it's bleeding.

(Gang fight over territory)

Greta: Here they come now, Gregory. Hold this wire to trip Brady. I'll pour dirty rainwater on them. For starters.

Brady Birch: I'm soaked. It stinks. Babs, I think we're getting the upper hand. I've twisted my ankle. Our Reds gang will control this territory soon. It's beautiful for us— not them.

Babs Birch: You weak-bellied Devils. See what you can do with this sticky tree sap (pours *brown sap on the ground)*.

Gregory: Careful, Greta. Our old friends are trying to get us stuck. My feet...messed up.

Greta: I'll create footprints. Lead them into their own trap.

Gregory: They want to control our hood, but they can't outsmart us.

Brady Birch: Control this land, or else—*(gang members comfort each other)*. We won't follow the trail. End up surrounded. Caught. We're not fools. Here come the cops *(some pushing and shoving. Police stop it)*.

Gregory: My arm is bleeding. Someone cut me. You'd better watch out, Brady. We'll get you. Wait and see.

47

Babs Birch: Brady and I will help you, Gregory. Stay calm. We've been wrong about so much. We were friends before this. Gangs hurt people and destroy property.

Scene 5

Birch Home

Ma Birch: Gregory, glad you are here while your arm heals. You kids have always been friends. Glad they brought you here…when you were hurt. We called your parents *(examines cuts and bandage).*

Pa Birch: Why did you kids choose gangs?

Gregory: My arm is not so sore now. Our gang really hasn't accomplished much. You Reds are just like us Devils in so many ways.

Pa Birch: So why do you fight…hurt each other…do those awful things?

Ma Birch: Yes, why do it?

Gregory: I'm going to stop *(long pause).* I'll help others, like you've helped me. Devils and Reds should be friends. I've thought about gangs…how bad they can be. We were wrong. We were wrong.

Pa Birch: There are other groups—better groups---to belong to. And other things—better things to believe in. Please talk to Babs and Brady about quitting the Reds. We're going to have a council of parents and neighbors at our home tomorrow.

(Council meets)

Pa Grayson: Parents, friends, neighbors, we have a serious problem here.

Ma Birch: Our children have drifted into angry gangs. Out of control. Harming others.

Pa Birch: This has to stop.

Pa Grayson: Last night, they battled over a piece of land. It soon will become a shopping mall. Neither gang has it.

Ma Grayson: We've got to turn these kids around. Tough love is in order. Each family must play a stronger role—more meals together, and conversations about future goals and careers.

Ma Birch: We can offer better options—job training, recreational centers, volunteer work, improved policing.

Pa Birch: We can do this. We can show our kids there is a better way. College for those who want it. Career training for those who don't—maybe community college for technical programs.

Pa Grayson: Gregory, how will you change?

Gregory: I'm so happy, so very happy. I'll be a person. I've quit the Devils. I'll get Greta to quit, too. We scare people, we hurt others, we damage the environment. We wreck other homes. Bad injuries and even deaths have been due to our gang warfare. I'll give talks and speeches to young people. I'll have a conference, a big meeting, with parents and teachers, and young kids, to show them the right way to live in peace. I'll be a role model and a counselor. Help others with their education, their careers, and hot to be good members of families and society. I'm a new Gregory! *(tears off and throws away gang insignia)*. That ring in my nose is gone, already.

(Ma and Pa Grayson cry and hug Gregory and Greta).

Greta: Me, too, Gregory.

Scene 6

Conference room

Gregory: This is the official start of the "Devils-Reds Annual Conference to End Gangs."

Greta: I'm so proud of my brother. I'm no longer a Devil. Not good for any of us.

Oliver Towles: As the police chief…too good to be true. Things don't change, suddenly, like this. Gang leaders will forget it. We need more police involvement *(puffs up chest)*.

Pa Grayson: You're right, Chief. We also need a "tough love" approach. If they don't behave and fly right, they're…

Ma Grayson: That might just force them into gangs.

Oliver Towles: It might force them into appropriate behavior. Rejoin the community *(shines his badge with handkerchief)*.

Gregory: Greta, please read the quotes from the detention center—a prison for teens.

Greta: "See these tattoos on my arms—roses and sharp claws? We were gang-bangers. We hurt girls in other gangs. Our own, too. Now we live in this dump." And "Our gang went after all kinds of kids. We hurt and scared as many as we could. We felt good about belonging to something that was powerful. We were accepted. We cared about each other. We had secret codes and secret handshakes."

Scene 7

Conference room

Oliver Towles: This thing has gone far enough. It's got to stop. I'm sending them to prison—the whole lot.

Pa Birch: You've got our complete support, Chief. Whatever you think is best.

Devils Leader: We'll stop, I promise. We'll break up our gang. We're in too much trouble.

Reds Leader: We will, too. We'll cool it. We want to live.

Oliver Towles: Can I trust you both? Will you turn in your gang insignia and body-rings? Let skin heal, and have your tattoos removed?

(Devils Leader and Reds Leader nod heads in unison).

Oliver Towles: I'll let anyone going to prison, or in prison, for a non-felony, gang-related offence, go to the Army, Navy, Marines, or Air Force (laughs). If they'll have you, that is.

Gregory: While they disband, the Devils and Reds can still compete.

Oliver Towles: How can they?

Gregory: Well, Chief, they can see which group raises more money for the Youth Center.

Oliver Towles: Great idea. The police will gladly help (straightens his tie).

Devils Leader: We'll call it the Gregory Grayson Center for Youth.

Reds Leader: For recreation and sports. Education and jobs. Positive individual development.

Gregory: Thank you so much (walks away, slowly, to hide his tears).

War and School

A Play for Young Teens

by

Norman and Jane Giddan

CAST

Farouk Sabbati – Father

Fatima Sabbati – Mother

Farid Sabbati – Son – age 15

Falita Sabbati – Daughter – age 13

Carl Cohen, M.D.

Pa Grayson – Hotel manager and teacher

Ma Grayson – Hotel business manager and teacher

Gregory Grayson – Son – age 15

Greta Grayson – Daughter – age 13

SETTINGS

Scene 1   Apartment in hotel

Scene 2   Apartment in hotel

Scene 3   Apartment in hotel

Scene 4   School

Scene 5   School

Scene 6   Neurologist's office

Scene 7   Rehab Center

Scene 8   Hotel Lobby

Scene 1

Apartment in hotel

Pa: Welcome to our hotel, my new friends. You have traveled far...must be tired and relieved.

Ma: You are safe here at our Bungalow Hotel. Far from the bombings and devastation in Syria.

Pa: Farid and Falita can go to our one-room schoolhouse. Here at the hotel.

Ma: They will study with our own kids, Gregory and Greta. About the same age.

Fatima: We feel so fortunate to be here. *(yawns).* God has been good to us. Thank you.

Farouk: It's been a long journey. We have much to share. Much that you might not believe *(closes eyes as if in prayer).*

Fatima: We are so grateful for your kindness.

Farouk: God will help us overcome our many problems. We are without any of our possessions. We have no way to repay your generosity *(bows slightly).*

Fatima: And our children are still very unsettled by the war...especially Farid *(wipes her eyes with scarf).*

Farouk: Food was so scarce that many people were lost.

Pa: Sleep here. Eat what you want. We have whatever you need. Local charities help support you.

Ma: We're family. Don't worry about a thing. You owe us nothing.

Scene 2

Apartment in hotel

Gregory: Pa, look how many people have offered to participate in a fundraiser…so generous.

Greta: The raffle for the platters of chocolate covered seeds is a good idea, Middle-Eastern delicacies tempt…all of us.

Gregory: Look at the offers for food supplies, utensils. Even babysitting services. The hotel residents…are great.

Farouk: My wife and I are very moved…everyone's thoughtfulness. The memory of wartime death and destruction is still fresh in our minds. Our hearts are stirred by your generosity.

Fatima: We escaped after a close call with an IED bomb. No peace.

Falita: The bombs were horrible, so horrible.

Farid: Several were very close to…*(walks away)*.

Scene 3

Apartment in hotel

Fatima: So quiet around the hotel on the weekend. Thank you for inviting us for tea *(stirs spoon in cup)*.

Farouk: The children are playing soccer together. Without fighting—for the moment.

Pa: Quite an outburst from Farid the other day. What do you think it was about?

Farouk: He just seems to erupt like a volcano. No apparent reason. We think it's an after-effect of the bombings near him.

Fatima: He doesn't sleep very well. Awakens with nightmares. In fact, we all do, some nights.

Ma: I know your doctor in Syria told you not to worry about him...these symptoms sound serious. Let's get him examined again *(eyes show concern and love)*.

Pa: Here's the number of our friend, Dr. Carl Cohen. He's a pediatric neurologist...could tell you more about what's going on with Farid. Give him a call.

Farouk: We'll do that. Things just don't seem to be getting any better for Farid. He's struggling at school *(dark eyes squint with worry)*.

Fatima: God willing, we would love to get some help for him. Thank you *(holds Ma's hand in gratitude and kisses her on both cheeks)*.

Ma: Perhaps an education plan would help.

Fatima: I'm still very worried about Farid. He has much more of a problem than the Syrian doctor thought. Anything else to be done? You've been so wonderful to us.

Ma: We can make him a separate study booth to block out distractions. That should allow him to focus on his worksheets more easily *(draws booth with her hands in the air)*.

Pa: He forgets the instructions we give him. How about a little notepad and pencil, so he can write down what he hears? Then he can check his own notes. Follow directions better.

Farouk: It's probably not enough to cure him, is it? We'll need to know more about his mind and how it works.

Ma: We've noticed Fatima gets dizzy now and then. Sometimes can't recall things—like amnesia. Only for certain times or things.

Fatima: She needs help, too. God will do what's right for us *(holds out arms with palms up)*.

Scene 4

School

Ma: Children, we have two new students with us today. They have flown for thousands of miles...escape the warfare in Syria *(points with palm up at new students).*

Pa: We hope...please be considerate as they get used to their new home. To our classroom.

Ma: Gregory, will you come to the board and show the class how you did the first algebra problem?

Pa: Farid, let me know if you have any trouble with these. Did you work on problems like these at your old school?

Farid: *(sits stone still and doesn't respond).*

Ma: Let's give him more time, Pa.

Pa: Take you time, Farid *(walks to him and pats him on the shoulder).* Maybe "show and tell" will be a more relaxed time.

Ma: Falita, would you and Farid like to show us or tell us something about your country? None of us has ever been to the Middle East.

Falita: *(stands up, lowers her eyes).* I am from Damascus in Syria *(long pause).* Once a very beautiful city. Green palm trees and bright gardens were everywhere *(starts to sweat and quake as her voice cracks).*

Farid: *(stands up slowly, breathes hard).* War has ruined everything. We lost many friends. We can never go back.

(After class, enter Sabbati parents).

Ma: Oh, dear. Your children have been through so much. There must be something we can do to help your family.

Pa: We've planned a fund-raiser. Invite everyone at the hotel—and the neighbors.

Farouk: You are so generous. How can we ever repay you? *(shakes hand with Ma and Pa).*

(Next day)

Farid: You little nothing. I hate you. I could kill you *(punches Gregory's arm).*

Gregory: Let me go. Let me go. You'll smother me. I can't breathe.

Farid: We're brave hunters. My forefathers trained birds of prey—taught falcons to kill. Return to them *(bends elbow, as if to hold a falcon)*.

Gregory: I don't care. I didn't do anything to you. You're crazy.

Ma: Enough, you guys. Settle down. No more squabbling.

Pa: Yes, this is a classroom. *(yells)*. Stop it or get out of here. You are both suspended from school for one day.

Gregory: That's not fair. Farid started it. It's his fault.

Farid: For a moment, I was back in Damascus *(hides face in hands)*.

Scene 5

School

Pa: Hey guys. Farid seems kind of lost in our class. He's scary and unusual. Maybe we can help him.

Greta: Gregory could be his buddy in class.

Ma: Good. I could print up a schedule, so he'll know what's coming next.

Greta: He doesn't remember our names. Could make sticky nametags for ourselves.

Falita: Those are great ideas to help Farid. Thank you. Thank you. He'll really like that. I'm glad you don't hate him.

(Boys return to school)

Farid: I'm sorry I yelled at you.

Gregory: Whatever, Farid. It's hard to start in a new place. Let's shake and be friends *(extends his hand to Farid, who shakes it).*

Ma: Time to get to work on your compositions. Farid, what's wrong?

Farid: *(mumbles with his head down on the desk)* Mrs. Grayson, I have a bad headache. I can't write anything.

Ma: Come and lie down on the couch in the rear *(she helps him to the couch, he lies down, she covers him and sits down beside him).* Are you comfortable?

Farid: *(rubs fingers on couch)* The couch feels soft. Each time I close my eyes…fire and hear the loud IED explosion. As if they were happening again.

Ma: No wonder you're having trouble concentrating. You poor thing. It must have been terrible for you.

Farid: I think I can rest now *(closes eyes and dozes off).*

Scene 6

Farid and Falita are referred to a pediatric neurologist

Dr. Cohen: *(sits on edge of desk)* You've got a wonderful son and daughter, Mr. and Mrs. Sabbati.

Fatima: Thank you, doctor. What's wrong with them?

Dr. Cohen: They both have what we call TBI, "traumatic brain injury." Brought on by the bombings and explosions in Syria.

Fatima: They were never shot or cut or wounded. They didn't even bleed.

Dr. Cohen: Yes, but their brains were injured. Swelling and shrinking after the blast. Thank goodness they were no closer than they were.

Farouk: Farid must have been close. What can we do now?

Dr. Cohen: I've prepared a list of strategies that may help at home and at school. I'll give you several copies.

1. Keep life simple.
2. Provide more quiet time for studying.
3. Write lists for important things.
4. Try books on tape.
5. Use spell-check and grammar-check on a computer.

Fatima: Thank you, doctor. We can do those things. Right away. Today.

Dr. Cohen: And I'm prescribing some pills. Will help them both sleep better at night. I want them to come to my rehab center as soon as possible. *(Shakes hand with parents as a way to cement the agreement).*

Farouk: Of course, they'll come.

(Sabbatis talk as leave office)

Farouk: It's a relief to talk with someone who understands, isn't it? I wish we'd seen him back home *(shakes head slowly).*

Fatima: Yes, Dr. Cohen's advice is very valuable—and very expensive.

Farouk: Oh yes. The bills. Nothing short of a miracle will get us through this financial nightmare.

Fatima: Hardly a nightmare, compared to what we've lived through. God willing, we'll find a way. We'll find a miracle.

Scene 7

Treatment at the rehab center for Farid and Falita by Dr. Cohen

Dr. Cohen: Welcome, young Sabbatis, to our rehab center. Others have similar problems. Many with even more visible and serious injuries.

Falita: I'm scared, doctor.

Dr. Cohen: *(holds Falita's hand)* Don't be. We'll go slowly. We'll just start with word games this morning designed to help your conceptual learning.

Farid: What's "conceptual learning?"

Dr. Cohen: Well, in simple terms, it's about using language to create and understand ideas. Your speech therapist will show you what I mean. She'll help you learn new words…talk about word meanings. She'll group words or pictures together. Even create short stories with you.

Farid: Will we have games to play to help us remember things? My parents love to play games at home. So do we.

Dr. Cohen: Yes, I'll make sure you have plenty of games.

Farid: I like it here, already. So does my sister. We'll work hard here and try to get better very fast *(high-fives Dr. Cohen)*.

Scene 8

Bungalow Hotel Lobby.

A 10K race is planned by the Graysons to raise money for the Sabbatis. Several hundred people will pay ten dollars each to participate in the race. They get a gift basket with bottled water to use during the race. The Graysons and Sabbatis are utterly amazed by the response of those staying at the Bungalow Hotel, as well as hundreds of others.

Pa: Ma, I have an idea to help the Sabbatis with their medical bills. We'll launch a 10K race. Start here at Bungalow. Invite people from far and wide.

Ma: A great idea, Pa. We can charge admission. I can assemble gift baskets for all the participants...treats and bottled water.

Pa: I'll notify runners and marathoners — they'll come.

Ma: I'll inform the media. Quite an event. *(She hugs and kisses Pa).* Now I know why I married you.

(One month later)

Pa: *(Speaking on a bullhorn).* The Bungalow Hotel 10K race is about to begin. Hundreds of you have assembled for a good cause. Good luck in the race.

Gregory: Greta, have you ever seen so many runners in one place? This is amazing.

Greta: Never so many here. It's not Boston or New York. Cameras are clicking and popping everywhere. What a turnout!

Gregory: Ma, let me taste some of the treats when we put together the gift baskets. They are delicious *(smacks his lips).*

Greta: What a great way to help the Sabbatis pay off their medical bills.

Gregory: They're off!

Farouk: The race was so exciting. Many hundreds of runners. We raised enough money to fund our Foundation for TBI for a year. We're so grateful…to this entire community.

Fatima: We're doubly blessed. Our children have shown so much improvement from the treatment at Dr. Cohen's rehab center.

Ma: We're giving Dr. Cohen and his staff a big grant from the TBI Foundation for their research *(Gregory and Greta hug her).*

Pa: We shall also honor all the individuals who are still suffering with the war—those who can't leave yet *(Gregory and Greta hug him).*

Dr. Cohen: You're right. Farid and Falita have improved. We've been honored and Ma and Pa are celebrated "teachers of the year." Remember those, on all sides, who've died, or been imprisoned, or tortured as a result of the Syrian War. They must not be forgotten—ever.

Fatima: Ma and Pa, you've been so wonderful. Here's an antique silver goblet from the glory days of our country, as a gift of thanks. We have a remarkable history.

(A welcome surprise to all, Farid and Falita walk through a side door, and enter the party. Applause and cries of joy, as they are recognized by the guests).

Farid: I can't thank you enough, everyone. Falita and I feel much better. More sure of ourselves. We're beginning to cope better with the effects of the war. America is a great place. We'll be able to return to school very soon. We knew what war was. Now we know what peace is. We'll be good students and good members of our family.

Falita: And what love is, too.

Grackles of Green Grove Meet Bird Boy

by

Jane and Norman Giddan

CAST

Audie Bahn	8 year- old boy with autism
Mom	Siena Bahn, 38 years old, Audie's mother
Dad	Bailey Bahn, 40 years old, Audie's father
Ma Grackle	Brown/black iridescent black bird
Pa Grackle	Iridescent black bird
Gregory Grackle	Son of Ma and Pa; Brother of Greta
Greta Grackle	Smaller iridescent bird; Sister of Gregory
Grackle Flock	Birds who live in the woodland
Several adults	Birders who accompany Mr. & Mr. Bahn

SETTING

Autumn in a small Midwestern town

MUSICAL SONG/POEMS

IN MY ROOM	Audie
CLOUDS	Audie
STORM	Audie
HAPPY IN THE WOODS	Audie
TUNNEL	Audie
FINALE	Audie

ACT 1

Scene 1

Setting: Audie, a 10-year-old boy with autism is in his room. His dresser is in view.
Toy cars and trucks are around him.

Audie becomes upset when he notices that one of his parents has altered
his universe by moving his favorite toy bird from its designated position on
his dresser. Audie, lining up his toys, pauses to look up at his dresser,
then gets upset when he sees his bird missing. He starts humming,
rocking and shaking his hands.

MOM

Audie, is that you getting all upset? Try to calm down. Here, I'll help you do your slow
breathing. *(They breathe together, counting to ten).* Now you can read from your poem
book.

AUDIE

Birdie gone *(desperately).* All gone *(points to empty place on his dresser).*

MOM

No Audie, Birdie's not gone. I just had to wash it. It will be dry soon and I'll put it right
back on your dresser where you can see it. In the meantime, why don't we hang up one
of the drawings you made of your bird, so you have a picture of Birdie to look at?

(She walks him out of his room, towards the porch.)

Come on out and swing on the porch while you wait. You always feel better when
you're outside near nature. Let me know if you see any of your favorite grackles today.

69

(She goes back into the house).

(Alone and calmer, Audie recites to himself).

AUDIE

IN MY ROOM–SONG/POEM

In my room, my personal space
Alone with myself, in my special place

My quiet spot, away from all noise
A time to line up all my favorite toys.

Uh oh. Oh no
Something is out of place

Uh oh, I feel pricklies
Squeezing on my face

I need to have order
Each thing in its spot

Or else my world topples
My head feels so hot.

70

ACT 1

Scene 2

Setting: Porch of the house. Woods sand meadow beyond. Porch swing in view.

Audie on the porch, looking skyward, calms himself by reciting an inventory of his cloud knowledge.

MOM

(Leading Audie to the porch swing.)

 Come on out and swing on the porch while you wait for Birdie to dry. You always feel better when you're outside watching the woods and the sky. Let me know if you see any of your favorite grackles today.

AUDIE

CLOUDS–SONG/POEM

Oh to fly way up high in the sky
Toward the clouds, far from clouds, nothing loud

Clouds are such a nice preoccupation
Changing shapes as breezes blow them by

When I feel a worry or anxiety
I watch cloud shapes floating in the sky

71

Thermal forces pulling warm air upward

Toward white cumulus gathering way up high

Nimbus is when cumulus turns inky

Warns me that a storm is gonna cry.

Cirrus are the puffs that look like cotton

Calm me on this peaceful sunny day

I see shapes in every cloud formation

Watching, looking, that's my kind of play.

DAD

Hey pal, you look lost in those clouds. Your mom and I have a treat planned for you.
We know how much you love birds…and your teachers want us to help you to follow
your interests…so I've bought us some bird books and binoculars…and signed us up
with the local birding club. We're going bird watching!

ACT 1

Scene 3

Setting: A grassy field at a nature preserve with woods in the distance.

Mom Dad and Audie in a grassy field at a nature preserve along with other bird watchers. As Mom and Dad observe birds through their binoculars, and comment on them, Audie wanders away. He follows an iridescent grackle that swoops down near him and leads him into the woods.

MOM

 This is called "birding," Audie. Your teachers will be happy we let you do this. We look at all different kinds of birds through these — binoculars

AUDIE

Noc-lars. Big eyes.

MOM

Yes, dear. They make things far away look bigger. Here, try these.
        (She helps Audie look through binoculars).

DAD

We can watch the birds flying, observe them eating, see their nests and even hunt for their eggs. All the things you like to draw, Audie.

AUDIE

Feathers, rainbow feathers.

MOM

Mom: Yes, Audie we will see lots of pretty feathers. Sit down on our blanket while we spot something for you to see.

(Mom and Dad both look through their binoculars, not noticing that an iridescent grackle swoops nearby and Audie starts to follow it).

MOM

Dear, this is perfect for Audie. He'll love seeing all his favorite birds in these fields and in the forest.

DAD

This is just what his teachers had in mind. We can identify the birds here, take photos of them, and then Audie can draw pictures of them to his heart's content.

MOM

Look dear, I see a flock of migrating grackles. They must be heading down from the north. They'll probably settle down here, lay their eggs, and raise their young. We can watch their progress every week, when we come back here. Quick, get Audie and show him. They are his favorite birds.

DAD

Audie…Audie where are you?

(He looks around their immediate area, furtively).

MOM

Oh no, where has Audie gone? (*Alarmed*).   Help everyone…(*Pleading*). Our son has wandered off…we've lost our son…(Shouting anxiously through her tears). Help us find him right away. Has anyone seen a boy wearing a forest green shirt and brown pants?

ACT 1

Scene 4

Setting: The autumnal woods

Audie follows the grackle into the woods, the flock's migratory habitat,
where the grackles build nests and develop community. The Grackle
family, Gregory, Greta Ma and Pa greet him. All the grackles forage for
feathers and leaves. They find a wide variety, with many different colors,
and attach them to Audie. Greta presents a leaf full of seeds and nuts, but
Audie simply arranges them in patterns on the ground. All the grackles
work together to gather leaves, twigs and straw to make a large nest on a
tree stump for Audie. Audie climbs in. Grackles are in boughs of threes,
encircling Audie, to protect him while he sleeps.

                              AUDIE

Shiny feathers

                              GRETA

Who are you?

                              AUDIE

Birds. Rainbow birds.

                           PA GRACKLE

Grackle: What's your name?

                              AUDIE

Bird.

75

GREGORY

He says he's a bird. We'll have to call him Bird Boy.

(Audie smiles).

GRETA

Bird Boy, you followed me to our new home. Shouldn't you go back to your parents?
You must be lost.

AUDIE

Birds… feathers… clouds… water rainbows (He hums happily and jumps up and down
with excitement). Mine. Mine.

GREGORY

He's very strange. Doesn't seem to hear what we say. Maybe he hit his head. Maybe
he's sick.

GRETA

Maybe he's from another planet.

PA GRACKLE

If Bird Boy stays here, he will need our help, no matter what. We must camouflage him
so he will blend into the woods and be safe, until his family finds him.

GREGORY

(Gathering feather and leaves and putting them on Audie).

Let's find feathers on the forest floor and put them on him. We'll dress him up like a
beautiful bird. Red, yellow, green feathers and leaves. Then he can hide here with us.

MA GRACKLE

He will need to eat. Set out some seeds for him.

(Greta fills a leaf with seeds and nuts, and places it before Audie).

GREGORY

(Very deliberately making pictures on the ground with the seeds and nuts).

Look, he's making pictures with our seeds. That looks like Pa Grackle, and there's a cloud shape. Why Bird Boy is an artist!

MA GRACKLE

He will eat when he gets hungry. In the meantime, we must make him a nest, so he will sleep comfortably while he's here.

(Grackles gather leaves, twigs, reeds and straw and proceed to make a large nest on a tree stump).

AUDIE

Rainbow feathers, sunny weather. Quiet stream. That's my dream.

ACT 2

Scene 1

Setting: Woodland area. Artwork by Audie, drawn and painted on bark, hangs from tree branches. Each depicts a different weather condition. A large green berry bush is nearby.

Audie explores the woodland setting. He reacts to colors, light through branches, sunlight glinting off puddles, clouds and reflections. Grackle family, Ma, Pa, Gregory and Greta are puzzled and confused by Audie's behavior. His verbal responses are cryptic and lack necessary information. Storm sounds, thunder, lightning soon begin.

MA GRACKLE

What should we feed him? Here, Bird Boy, try some worms and bugs that we eat.

AUDIE

Mmmm. More, more. *(He smiles with a mouthful).*

PA GRACKLE

Don't eat those berries. *(He points to a large green bush).* They make us sick.

GRETA

Do you think he comes from an egg like we do?

GREGORY

I don't know, but he sure is different from us. Did you see him on the telephone wire last evening? He didn't get the idea at all. Couldn't he see that we're all supposed to turn the same way? There he was sideways, while we all faced south.

GRETA

And in the wind this morning? There we were, each on a branch, face to the breeze, wings at our sides, while he stretched tall and spread those colorful feathers for all to see.

GREGORY

I don't know. He is unusual. See him staring at the clouds reflected in that puddle? *(He points to Audie, bending over a puddle, transfixed)*. He seems to be entranced by the sunlight.

GRETA

He is studying it carefully. Maybe he's getting ready to draw again. He is an amazing artist. Weren't you surprised when he drew that beautiful sunbeam, and the next day was bright and sunny as we built our nests?

GREGORY

Then he painted a cloudy day picture, and sure enough, there followed a gray, overcast day…just right for egg-laying.

PA GRACKLE

That Bird Boy sure has a knack for forecasting the weather.

MA GRACKLE

And a wonderful talent for drawing what he sees.

GREGORY

He looks like he's studying those cloud formations. I wonder what he's thinking now.

AUDIE

(Looking up at the birds and making a loud whooshing noise.)

GREGORY

What's that Bird Boy?

AUDIE

Wind blow. Wind pushing.

GRETA

He's drawing with a stick. What is that shape? A cloud — a big cloud and now he's darkening it with that burnt stick.

GREGORY

What's that Bird Boy?

AUDIE

Nimbus cloud. Big wind. Sky crying.

PA GRACKLE

Why that's a storm cloud. (*His voice gets louder, with urgency*). He's warning us about a big storm. Here comes that wind now.

(*Wind, thunder and lightning begin in the distance*).

MA GRACKLE

He's been right every day, so far. I trust what he's telling us. We must protect the eggs!

AUDIE

STORM–SONG/POEM

There's nimbus in the sky
The winds are swirling round
The sky is gonna cry
Get ready for that sound

I hate that thunder roar
The lightning scares my chest
But I have warned the birds
They need to guard their nests.

We're getting chilled and wet
Our feathers matted down
We need a sheltered place
That's safely underground.

ACT 2

Scene 2

Setting: Storm brewing in the forest. Large Oak tree in foreground.

Rainbow begins to form slowly, and wind kicks up. Sounds of adults

beating the bushes and underbrush; staccato screams of "Audie, Audie,

where are you? Are you here? Can you hear us?" Grackles huddle

around Audie who sits carefully camouflaged, with his back against an old

oak tree. Pa is perched on a limb above Audie.

MA GRACKLE
Audie…is that your name? They're calling you. They want you home now.

PA GRACKLE

(Perched on a limb above Audie).

Don't you want to go home? Your family wants you back.

GRETA

I'll feel so sad if you leave. Stay, Bird Boy, we want you to stay here. *(She begins to cry).*

GREGORY

It's so nice to have a visitor.

MA GRACKLE

What are you saying, my children? This boy needs to go home.

ASSEMBLED GRACKLES

(Chanting together)

Stay Bird Boy stay. Stay Bird Boy. Don't go away. Stay. Stay. Stay.

AUDIE

My rainbow birds.

HAPPY IN THE WOODS–SONG/POEM

I hear many voices

Weave in the wind

I'm near the birds singing

Don't want this to end.

My rainbows on feathers

My sun in the pond

My clouds changing weather

This has to go on.

Back home among people?

They want me, I know

But here in the forest

I feel all aglow.

ACT 2

Scene 3

Setting: Underground birding observation tunnel at edge of the woods

Grackles carry nests from tress and hand them to Audie who places them

in a safe underground tunnel, so the eggs will survive the hurricane.

GRETA

You're so strong. You can carry so many nests at once.

GREGORY

Yes, Bird Boy, we couldn't do this without you. You're a hero to us.

AUDIE

TUNNEL–SONG/POEM

Here comes the hurricane

We've got to move right now

Here, let me lead the way

We'll save the eggs, somehow.

We'll be safe from the storm

The eggs can hatch unharmed

I'm Bird Boy the new hero

I sent the storm alarm.

84

PA GRACKLE

You didn't go home, Bird Boy. You stayed to help us.

MA GRACKLE

We'll always remember you. Always. But your family must be very worried. They're trying hard to find you.

AUDIE

Bird Boy here. *(He flaps his arms, repeatedly, as if they were wings).*

ACT 2

Scene 4

Setting: The opposite end of the bird-watching tunnel

Audie's parents, caught in the torrential rains, find shelter in the
opposite end of the same bird-watching tunnel. All are safe, but
Audie is "alone" between the two worlds, holding his ears and
rocking as the storm crashes above. Parents notice Audie,
camouflaged like a bird, in the tunnel and rush toward him. He
looks beautiful to them and they embrace him, but he pulls away
and moves toward the birds.

MOM

Oh, my word! There he is…dressed up like a bird.

(*Sobbing, his parents rush towards him. They admire and embrace him,*

but he pulls away, and moves toward the birds).

AUDIE

I go. Bye-bye, my birds. Bye-bye my…. friends.

MOM

We're so happy to find you again, Audie. We've looked for days and had search parties
cover the area.

DAD

We knew you'd turn up, son. We hoped you weren't hurt or alone somewhere. You
look great!

AUDIE

Birds...feathers....Sky cry....boom.

MOM

Yes, we saw that storm, Audie. It made us worry so about you. I wonder how you stayed safe.

DAD

We got a telescope for you. (*Persuasively, for he's fearful Audie might leave again*). You can see even more than birds and clouds. You can see the stars and comets way up in the sky. Higher than the clouds.

AUDIE

Up, up, up?

MOM

Yes, dear. Way up in the sky. Far from here.

(*Mom and Dad embrace*).

ACT 2

Scene 5

Setting: The grackle compound in the woods

The eggs crack open. Grackles have been saved.

PA GRACKLE

He left me a poem. It says "Page 37. Eggs survive, babes arrive, all alive. Safe in nests, heads on chests, that's the best."

MA GRACKLE

He's such a caring and loving boy. He understood the eggs were our next generation and must be saved.

GRETA

He's a fine poet….and a talented artist.

GREGORY

He never said more than three words, but his drawings and his poems said it all for him.

GRETA

Maybe we could write music to go with his poems. Like an opera.

PA GRACKLE

Can birds write opera?

MA GRACKLE

Maybe they can, Pa, just maybe they can. They can try.

ACT 2

Scene 6

Setting: Clearing outside the tunnel

Bahn family walks out of the tunnel, all are crying.

DAD

What are you thinking, my son?

MOM

How have you been? Where did you live? How did my special Audie Bahn survive?

AUDIE

(Holding onto a hand of each parent, Audie sings/recites the finale).

FINALE–SONG/POEM

Back with my parents

Safe from all storm

Away from my feathered friends

But cozy and warm.

I love all of nature

Birds fascinate me

Clouds and reflections

Cause real ecstasy.

89

Lenses for watching

Nature afar

Markers for drawing

My birds, clouds and stars.

I've found my direction

I'll draw what I see

Studying nature

Naturally!!

THE END

To Parents, Teachers and Friends

In our story, Bailey and Siena Bahn have a son, Audie who has autism. The family goes birding, an activity recommended by Audie's therapists, to "follow his interests." Indeed, Audie is fascinated by things in nature: feathers and birds, and clouds. He spends most of his time looking skyward, reciting poems about nature and collecting bird memorabilia. On this particular outing, as his parents gaze through their binoculars, the boy wanders off, lured by an iridescent grackle.

Audie ends up in the midst of their flock and becomes a concern of the Grackle family, Ma, Pa Greta and Gregory, who take him under their wings, literally and figuratively, as they don't know how to find his home. They collect a great variety of feathers and leaves from the grounds around them and attach them to the boy, whom they call Bird Boy, so he will be safely camouflaged. While with the birds, he misinterprets their social signals, focuses on unexpected aspects of their real-life situations, and generally puzzles the flock, though they value his uniqueness. He displays various symptoms of autism, making them imagine that he has come from another culture, or.planet. They build him a nest and feed him various bugs, which he likes.

Audie's behavior seems quirky to the grackles. When they line up on their telephone wire, all in the same direction, he turns at a different angle. When they rest on every branch of a tree, all averting the wind in the same position, he lets the breeze separate his feathers, instead, in a beautiful display. Rather than eating it, he arranges birdseed on the ground in an array of cloud shapes, and gives each shape a name. He darkens the cumulus nimbus pictures with the charcoal tip of a burnt stick and recites an eerie and somber poem above them.

The Grackles begin to appreciate his knowledge of cloud formations and weather. On the day of spring hatchings, when all the delicate eggshells are about to open, he alerts the birds to an on-coming hurricane. He helps them carry their nests to a safe tunnel, protect their emerging young and they hail the boy as their hero.

As the storm clears, they end up in the birding tunnel where the boy's bereaved parents spot him. Adorned in feathers, he looks beautiful to them. They lure him back with a gift of his own telescope that will allow him to gaze afar at stars and comets high above the clouds, wind and rain.

Audie's actions help the birds to survive, and his parents to develop a new understanding of him. He is an artist and a naturalist. His poetry reveals his kind and sensitive heart. His social behavior may be awkward, but his artistic talent is powerful, as is his love of nature and the out-of-doors.

91

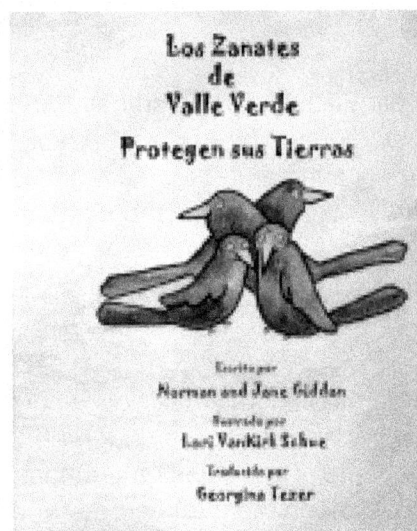

P.I.'s and police fight crime. Exciting, riveting mysteries and detective stories of revenge and redemption. A homeless shelter director murders volunteers. Gangs run wild in a dystopian future. Widow of a neurosurgeon with Alzheimer's seeks new life aboard a cruise ship. A transgender serial killer confesses...

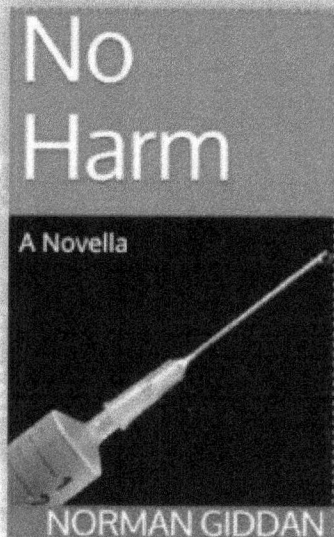

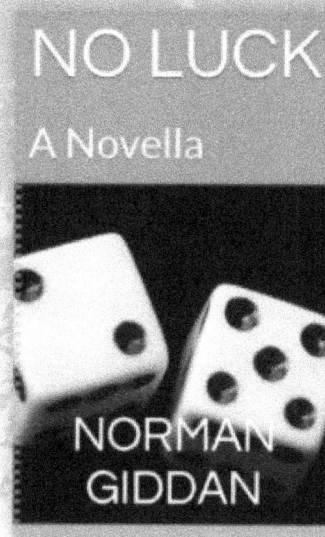